Rough Day

BOOKS BY ED SKOOG

Rough Day
Mister Skylight

Ed Skoog
Rough Day

COPPER CANYON PRESS
PORT TOWNSEND, WASHINGTON

Cover art: Photograph of Beth Henry Skoog and pet crow, 1939, Aspinwall, PA, taken by a relative.

Copper Canyon Press is in residence at Fort Worden State Park in Port Townsend, Washington, under the auspices of Centrum. Centrum is a gathering place for artists and creative thinkers from around the world, students of all ages and backgrounds, and audiences seeking extraordinary cultural enrichment.

LIBRARY OF CONGRESS CATALOGING-IN-PUBLICATION DATA

Skoog, Ed.
  [Poems. Selections]
  Rough day / by Ed Skoog.
     pages ; cm.
  ISBN 978-1-55659-434-2 (pbk. : alk. paper)
  I. Title.

  PS3619.K66R68 2013
  811'.6–dc23

                                        2013000952

98765432 FIRST PRINTING

COPPER CANYON PRESS
Post Office Box 271
Port Townsend, Washington 98368
www.coppercanyonpress.org

to Jill and Oscar

—

for Ben and for Catherine

ACKNOWLEDGMENTS

Parts of this book have appeared, often in a different form, in these magazines:

Acreage, The Adroit Journal, The American Poetry Review, Burnside Review, Cerise Press, Critical Quarterly, Cut Off Places, Dark Sky Magazine, Filter, Forklift Ohio, Gather Kindling, Gulf Coast, Hoarse, Jai-Alai Magazine, Los Angeles Review of Books, Narrative, The New Guard, New Orleans Review, PageBoy Maga-zine, Painted Bride Quarterly, Ploughshares, Poetry Northwest, Printer's Devil Review, Sixth Finch, Sonora Review, and *Tin House.*

"On river road" appeared, as "Trotline," in the Everyman's Library Pocket Poets anthology *The Art of Angling: Poems about Fishing,* edited by Henry Hughes.

Thanks to my father, my brothers, and my family-in-law.

Thank you Carolyn Hembree, David McAleavey, David Roderick, Faye Moskowitz, Gregory Pardlo, Heather Blasch, Jane Shore, James Hoch, Kary Wayson, Kevin Craft, Malachi Black, Matthew Dickman, Michael Dickman, Rebecca Hoogs, Rich Smith, and Yusef Komunyakaa for general assistance and/or reading these poems in process.

Support from Bread Loaf Writers' Conference, Idyllwild Arts Foundation, the Jenny McKean Moore Writer in Washington Fellow-ship at George Washington University, and Richard Hugo House gave me time, community, and encouragement to write this book. Thank you to the staff and supporters of Copper Canyon Press, par-ticularly Joseph Bednarik, Michael Wiegers, and Tonaya Thompson.

What I'm interested in doing is having a great time, and the audience having a great time, and living as long as I possibly can, and I'm as much in the dark about what happens after that as everybody else. Except I have a faith, which is, which is, which is, you know… it isn't anything to do with any particular people who… I mean, what's it all about? Why don't you tell me?

Shane MacGowan, interviewed in *MOJO,* February 2010

CONTENTS

Rough Day

ONE

What's in these books that have come to me

although they don't belong to me
I don't think

to whom then should they be delivered
also I don't know why
piled on the desk they came to me

mostly paperback

the books smell like someone's
house is burning in the dusk

it is like having been given a hand
no a shell
bone shards from the cemetery

at the end of the bus line to cemetery hill

for books are territory of the hand
these handed up by hands that shook my spine

what is in this body that has come to me
although I don't think it is properly mine
to whom should it be delivered

why to me I also don't know

by what design
as though at the end of another way

I've been given a footprint
to trap between my hands

A mile outside of Yellowstone

loose sky fallen into bruise
I put down my hitchhiking sign

wait for dawn at a gas station
I work mink oil into my boots
and talk about the early snows

sketch in ballpoint a stranger's face

on the last page of the book of elegies
I have been carrying around

I'm trying to find where influence end
a force emigrant in spirit
forget the old language

silent and defeated

to see the original inquiry was too small
a child passes into an empty house

passing into uncertain encounter
what will save me is the taste of miles
dirty under midnight's skillet

the west has helped me listen to myself
the west is a place that kills and kills and kills

What is silence for

wholly identical to itself
unless it find saltine night

or does it decide to belong
as if telephone wires were antlers
or an athletic portrait of calm

I was nothing coming into this name

like plastic it knows a way to die
goes under or becomes lit water

or whatever the dj calls
the nameless avenue that cuts

a long pillow again
sky's wet hard ancient feet

Rage: after the funeral

I spend a week with it
throw open and slam closed doors

the garden trellis a grotesque
tragedian on its fall stage
it roars

in the garage

I find no rake
only

the animal we hunt and avoid
silent in its cage

Our bare brief jeweled guitar

goes gone into bright
wilderness to write its own songs

a king carries groceries
along the frontage road
lickweed blooms in the yard

abandonment covers the house

I look up from work
what am I allowed to see?

close as heard rain
sharp as a closed knife
a condition of sorrow

forgotten in tallgrass rusts

a draft horse's iron shoe
my cure

You might have to

put down your money for a minute
because we have a custom

and the custom is

                              *

a glacier covers us tonight

midnight walks silver miles
and across barroom smoke I hear

a rough train bear scepter east

                              *

they put me to bed

I come back down to run between tables
mother why am I writing this poem

I am practicing that language of unfinishable sentences

who wants pancakes?
and what is this pancake to you?

What my mother loves is solitaire

and when her eyes start fading
to move about her house lights off

my brother is an orange
crate of records
on a car hood

playlist for silences ahead

my father is a plaid armchair that smokes
a tornado warning combs the elm

and after
my mother sets me adrift in the pool
with tennis racquet on yellow raft

to ferry small lives the storm washed in

identify by weight each feathered

furred alive or lifeless form
and dump out without decorum

Light chores between first and second sleep

she writes seven letters after dinner
counsels her children on what to avoid

naps beneath an oil of sea and cliff
rises to make coffee for neighbors
I keep lights low too now

it goes by too fast her age

she leaves no valediction
no shield

just still rooms
a green yard and a full pool

car wheels
counting bricks as they round the corner

Ice recoils tonight from marshes

bangs the set-out trash below my rental
cold and round already melting at my feet

hail breaks every pane I cover
with tape and cardboard
full sky turning blue over the rooftops

wet my cheek through broken glass

down in the garden pumpkins
lump their own hallucinations

sow thistle chickweed clover
broadleaf plantain
red-root amaranth

what was planted dies

any work of hands
only weeds keep growing

with moist matted prosperity

even the hour we abandon the garden
then the long winter

Meanwhile I am preparing

a way to miss the exiting animal
grizzly bear whooping crane

the slow hesitant and administrative desert tortoise
that I will probably outlive or my son will
already I see that my death

will or will not be like extinction

if only in the sense
that there was some noise and then there was no noise

yet why when I am grieving
do I insist the dead are inexact
without specifying how

extinction the bad trophy

and this is a good knot for holding a horse
and this is the desert's smell after a good rain

and here is the canyon where we stop for love
and these are the red and orange seeds of the ocotillo
and these are the spines of the pencil cholla

and here is the debris and here is the rain

and here is how to live with almost nothing
and beyond, even as the rattlesnake

takes its shade from my long standing

even as the tarantula goes to the highway
at sunset and is not struck

Some parts of speech are harder to draw

and yet to be really happy
beaten

and beaten
I must say my three lines
and wait beside the machinery

firing like a mind

watching
a fellow inmate run

cantering in that prison
without walls
forgiveness an insider

and has rascalled its steel

a disorder that tells you
when shadow rings

it destroys
is adolescent
says come out of the darkness

though from this angle I can't tell

whether it's the wind fussing its level

or I'm good at being a man
and what that would mean

One time I fell down got cut

got pushed down into a ringing in my ear
ringing that may be listened to

all I can tell you is my own experience
and don't want to get sideways with that power
there's no rain here

light's the same

have you ever been in an alley like that
compost and broken basketball hoop

punk gloom of after-party that breaks up at dawn
when the older boy sets a recliner on fire
breakfast comes differently after that

then children

her pulse beats under black concert T
stereo and gin on the other side

they find me in the barn half-asleep
where alley turns from road
loft hay bundled and forked becomes dust

attic curates a chain on a nail

aerial twitches through residual boards
I'm a hundred years from plough
that quartered here

dusky in the rafters: a sparrow

one's always nearby
someone's always nearby

TWO

At times I want to walk off the set of my body break my name and burn it

first rain fell hard
now how lightly

like the first
silences I had any right to survive
the first joys

close to the highway far from the on-ramp

elders argue in a bus stop crèche
one says to the other

I will not look at you

I will stab your
singing throat

Midnight radio from Astoria plays funk

I'm thinking about storms far out at sea
at the cabin table as songs end

and the needle taps against the marina
my wife sleeps
over her shoulder fishing boats

move miles bobbing lights adjust to roar

walking in the morning we find a speedboat
smashed on the feldspar of Lost Boy Bay

a weekender's aluminum toy
so may the dispatcher hear me
calling in the registration

I pause between each number
each letter

Let me try this clumsy again at dawn

casting knots that deform the current
concentric toward the zeppelin barn

not salmon but a kind of unemployment
I'm drawing
with three sides of the valley in my ear

my body a green overtone

how many nights within enormous hearing of the sea
how many exposures until I fail to comprehend

bramble against shoulder
catching thorn to rip flannel

each thought a rope to lash
a mattress on top of my car

The historical marker is a form of guilt

backward meaning
that might pull a muscle in your neck

adopting the historical posture
of the park ranger who rushes in
with scratches on his arm

dotted line of blood showing through his shirt

shows us reconstructed Acadian rooms
where things were done with bowls and linen

Europe discarded to various colonial rooms
forgotten in boxes
to build an outsider culture

that our ranger his mind still in last night's bed

recites glancing down at his cell phone
what is he supposed to do now

call the woman or man he just left and say
what then
probably all history is there

derange the language they once used

my mind in its cold migration
doesn't care where it lives

will always move between a series
of eleswheres latching satchel
hurrying over the bridge up

winding roads into the bamboo
vantage over whale-farted seas

The condo held the rock star's body like a puppet

and though it keeps small lawn
clean and circumspect as a crèche

when I walk past it coming home
from Blue Moon Tavern's oil
painting of Theodore Roethke

I quiet

the possibility to pass
unnoticed

to hover like a phrase…
I only am beginning to feel love
now that faces are slipping into disuse

and also how hate may be given unseen
and perhaps the work is to abandon it like a shelter

I haven't ruined my body yet with joy

though I worry it like a carpenter
working on a building for ghost

safety of rage
comfort in revenge
I once found them at the edge of song

fleeing the fire the cold either

I would give a full accounting of time
but cannot remember it

and anyway that world has passed us

except for antiques
college students smoking on a porch

Whatever I have been doing all my life I am doing now

here beneath the drop ceiling
a lost dancer an unemployed machinist

at the nameless house
edited from footage
we only live a moment

what the diorama excludes we may

be able to see
one another's pain over the waves under the cliff

body over thoughts of body and yet
one Wednesday I sold my car the one
my mother and father got lost in

coming back from the cemetery

her asleep in the backseat white-haired
eyeglasses in her hand

now I take to streets and slow Seattle down
I was a palace I was a forest
one scene and then another a son

whatever the word is for the living

suddenly alert and trying to get it all

down in playbill margins between changes
read it back to me

I'll try to stop singing

in the Saturn Bar's security-camera
grey and red neon

where Clouet crosses St. Claude
rattled corner hangs paintings by a hell-diver
who rose too fast into bent visions

he traded drinks for

acrylic-on-panel shrimpboats
bearing forward cursive in grand roving
the name *O'Neal*

who owns the bar and stands as the only

bartender since the fight
a jukebox warbles the damage inward

When word comes the emperor of the world has died

and lies in state at the old city hall
we join the flock and follow the body along

with five thousand others to the field
not the kind of funeral thrown
any doctor or lawyer

but for one who sings

personally in cape and wig
let mass grief give to mass joy

appearance and disappearance

afterward the colonel and I in seersucker
walk down to the magic show

a stage of blinds and screens
appearance and disappearance
a dove fluttering—voilà!—

vivid from assistant's cuff

to an assassin's velvet melody
and if one magician
crawl away in shadow

thinking himself unseen

so the empire is also gone
and the avenue escaping into the parish

those years these lines outstretched

lightweight and striped
fly from my sleeve

No longer a kid I have come to the grave

if it is—sign says not sure
what state is this

I have driven half-ashore the leather map
an every-Saturday parade of boxcars across a graveyard
some geography opened inside my storytelling

the iron fence is a paragraph

sign says you too I say the gun I found
in a sack of *National Geographic*

gun I counseled all year in my Army-Navy coat
cold water against my temple black night
pointed at the frenzy mute: whatever it thought

it never spoke its six bullets
soft ducklings behind their mother

You were beside me at the start of this

deserter
now I'm in the roadless area

asking water what it dreams of
predator of sadness
I would follow anyone

they are still there so am I

in the self-murdering bunker of my body
and as long as I have my body

they will be there cruel and guilty

I am least in love with error
those cold amendments

On river road the moon suspends

the catfish at human height
by telephone pole nail

the hammerer must have
come early to haul the trotline
bring that lord across water's blade

I held you farewell and loyal to hold

and still surge forward in my telling
replacing the spectacular with sad blackout

many bridges cross the Kaw
I carry one around

THREE

When I land and get in the taxi

I have to ask what the driver thinks my name is
because he says you're him

but not who
it's never cleared up
do you like fish he asks they have great fish

rounding the memorial his tape deck plays

navigating the detours around the mansion
his tape deck plays

pivoting around the museums and hotels
passing assassination and conspiracy
retracing the final parade of the army

his tape deck plays

some old piano music I like
trickling from return's edge

a song about the desire upon release
from prison to win the good return

Outside my apartment

snowdrifts surrender broken branches
inside I stand wet boots

soldierly against the plaster wall
everything's in the era where I left it
the fiddle the mail

window blinds still lowered against glare

my bed yet unmade

strangely peopled
with fine pillows not ours

Affixed to upper balconies of the World Bank

bolted-in speakers imitate seagull calls
a message to real seagulls about the arrangements

capital does and fails to concede
unless I do sums right I may hear
beyond invisible gulls

one star scraping against another

unless I permit myself to hear
clearly in the star-proofed capitol

I may turn into the instrument my pursuer
plays my own song upon
affixed to high eave

I tape gold stars on the news for this fever

I move into like a segment
World Bank is a reddening tomato

a burnt-clove smolder beyond the hill
laundry chemicals drift from rooms

beside the World Bank contractors' entrance
this language will be extinct in a hundred years

I'm in Washington and

it's January
in my abandoned coat

walking late at night
past the White House
a big piece of gravel

the past can drive itself to work

history although it may be small
is a bee trapped in a car

my advice is give yourself freely to rage
until your face suns in the blast of either
the furnace my grandfather stokes

or the revolver's answer

I become a man looking for work
a pilot looking for any onrushing place to land

Like a die that is only real every sixth throw

a bump under the century conceals my own child
who greets me from its face

a green grammar blooms in the snow
debonair in its whirl of reproduced
images so nearly oneself

this dash is formal fiat not formal activity

movement behind the thin curtain
a car door closing at three a.m.

*

after school at the gas station

muggery of nonsense night
is very pleasant and all year run

thick in summer a shock of wheat
it doesn't matter that you
were a gigantic child

back in the city with bigger whiskers

the lathe and plaster, always prepared
born and raised, gone away and come back—

*

helpless island with sand

gladden this final sound
may lead others to follow

where they can't go

back at the pasture
the police in my yard

*

you see them sometimes displeasing by highway

dripping ink into the grass
cinderblock hennaed with sayings

occluded, the regent turning away
indelicate alleys with cracked destination
door and gate, kicked mailbox, rattled fence

in nothing's costume

each morning someone's difficult
kiss the lake by surprise on either side

*

a figure swimming inside the waves

have to stay quiet to keep him singing
have to sing to keep him still

*

sleep grunts of stomach and throat

unarmed and heavily defended
high tide outside the oyster shed

footing and collapse here I saw

an image or an act, one or the other
itinerant in the reticulated dawn

Grizzled countenance of morning

leers in the apartment's slotted blinds
at leg and arm and face

I'm willing to confront it this morning
troughs run thick with sludge
junkyard piles higher

a kid goes into the water and walks out grown

tv says backgrounding breakfast and shower
and the intent quirking pulse up

after lunch is the end of a war
sluggish beauty moves universally on
holidays come kin collect take short walks

try to come to agreement about what's funny

try to construct a face from discarded materials
until desert debris becomes another you at last

my shelf of books wants to console me
but I feel like an exonerated murderer
with wince that the past is lost

an end of books ought to be a starting over

at a bookstore yesterday I saw an empty shelf
marked poetry and the loudspeaker said *finally*

I am a child of ghosts

so when these new ghosts come ashore in black boats
drag them up the sand

when they take occupancy in the abandoned house on the bluff
not even the baker's blind dog sleeps
I am a child ripening mischief in open cupboards

no one else knows this new ghost music

no one will tell them go away
no road between the dead's house

and the living road
keeping low I belly through tallgrass not breaking a stem
but closer to the house I tangle

vine drags my ankles thorn pulls my skin

I free myself toward the house
in the darkness that lives inside a drawer

the kind of night that worry is
but these through the lit window are not my ghosts
dancing nude around a bottle singing *wooky wooky*

I hurl fists of peat against the window but they keep dancing

I light some tinder and throw it against glass
but they keep dancing and the dance goes like this

His grin's upside-down police cruiser

and neck strain's tight as a hunter's field in fall...
somewhere in his visage a man sprays smoke over bee boxes

and when he talks I hear old sneakers tumbling dry
what happened to his Adam's apple
the black dog sits by the window

two flies circle
leaves land then anesthetized

pharmacists play cribbage winning and losing on the porch
a film comes on the television
there will be the usual headaches eviscerations

Gulliver attends his narrative on the mantel

painted on a delicate decanter
the box fan is plugged in but does not move

we ate deer and lemons in those days
we didn't love and became the past

salmon are moving towards extinction
my chair is from Sweden

Each friendly encounter is a basement

I may break my neck falling into
often too late I sense that someone beside me

has just stopped
crying or arguing a moment before
they keep me up the problems

every face is a gate with hinges

what moon and sun are I am also
as earth turn spit in cadence

oily rags burning or sweat-and-tobacco
you hear me we don't earn any money being lost
with this harm that seems a cover version of harm

let me open medicine cabinet mirrors to find

I'm unprepared—didn't prepare!
for only so far can I take you into the complicated interdealings

filling the night's prescription
red line station darkened by storm

I write her name on every napkin

I've never been farther from her
than a hand from what it's holding

yet may be turned into what I hunt

maybe through passage I become
a color photograph of a strip mall
become my sister in slow sheets

and I'm my body no more

eyelids where they meet are cold
news while space remains bottomless

what we could do is earn a bunch of guns

streaming a gasoline idea through waves
I have forgotten the order of

Money is a bandage where above the oak

blue absences arrive with gun-orange range
it soars tightly near the real subject

money's erotica that keeps promises
where it is always a winged inheritance
teaching survival along the bark's fissures

on Sunday I hunker down too

beside clean socks someone dropped by
among strange friends whose eyes

I recognize as more or less mine
powerfully
I've halfway died

unless it slips apart in secret

abandoned gesture of infinite alphabet
dollars step into the yard fat as gas cans

and badgers sleep beneath their throats
and whales fall disused into their trench

FOUR

My mother is a ferocity on the Hilton Hotel roof

a false falcon
skateboarders propelled by car mirror

glide past like ducks in migration
down at the harbor boats button up
a croaker throws green

body from iron water

mad saint's pink brain with terrible blue agency
it keeps me up the problem

written on the surface
what the boat and the fish and the splash are
my pulse is also

its own relic

moon spreads its bar cloth over the city
smoke fills the hotel room

a crumbled novel stoned and solved
from the plaza I hear interstate's small coffee
the farther I run from it

let me say this traveling's hard

plum blossoms cover the basketball court
foil from my shawarma falls to the floor

By now the hospital has unfolded

to the heavy planet of the wrecking ball
and I'm awful

driven to enter a broken door
pioneer mad abandoned hallways
curtains torn halfway off their institutions

my father was born in one of these rooms

and eighty years later
lives a block away

rusted file cabinets give me library
anthologies of modern literature
deeper files I dare open to cadaver

weathered on the roof I yell up god

watch the lost eagle follow the river west
I see what they are not why

against bright cloud they're headless
O for that
head and body gone off on their own

the chimney's great owl is only a wing

and coos when I take
flashlight up nightmare's stairway

just before I graduate and leave
the hospital is razed and I watch brick tumble
what has already become dust in me

whichever ghost follows me
stands shy on the stair

I am an event in my sudden willed loner's mute drama

unaudienced with a childishness that would light the town
with the last of my money I acquire a percolator

that drives a private silence through my sleep
which is a tunnel the moon trundles through
my apartment hallway carpet makes shadows like letters

have fallen among florets

people alone in their apartments sit up in bed
a child plays soldiers on the elevator

out my window I see where the houses drip into wheat
orange glow of the presidential library
I elevator to lobby its light in evening reduction

plaque that demands we remember the president stayed here

when he was no longer president
many absented spaces

I thought there was something of myself there
cement still warm from the afternoon

Last light of summer glints off the motorcade

strangers are in the house
crowding the beds

as if a horse has fallen asleep
I try to adjust minimally
forms barely seen are arousing

laughter behind a shower curtain

a car turns around on matinee road
I become a horseman of antecedent

and in my review go on to mention
deadening repetition and brutality
on another page

gentle little euphemism

debt that calls compassion to the mound
to talk it out

and talking
open myself to rain delay
say wait I have been given the wrong grief

we're in that area where people who can't get in go

I promise and lean into the punch

my old car ran on nothing but signs
my ships are iron and my face is gone

The stoned guy from the first floor

enunciates the broadcast in sterling
and waits inside the thought of the athlete

the way bottles are ghosts
of distant friends and eat raw
the lead mockery at the outset

morning light
the airfields at breakfast

How we tear the billboard down is how we tear the house down

you down me
each time I come home I fall apart

till continent hide and I stand birch
burn blade and yet when I suggest over toast
the president ought to be tried for war crimes

my father over eyeglasses says
that's not how grown-ups talk

the solider says being a soldier
is always having a place to run in place
it is flat's collapse

and when war shakes loose from fate's longest tailfeather

first job's feel stone turn cold under palm
rather be a tractor like a marble bust's churning

shoulder and a man inside the face
steps down from machine goes in for lunch
yet from where I stand mind's a claw

in that difficult library that lends

I struggle with myself of course
I struggle with these lines

tying to yoke together
the ox of meaning and the other one

John Donne was dean of St. Paul's

born a girl I'd have been Pauline
it's good to hear your other name

names are of interest
doors we pass through to break down
side doors are usually the best way

a series of interrogation rooms

this short curriculum
with the sacked city we are always fleeing

bright on our backs
to make from debris a new thing
it makes me think of my other life

this minor chord

if I step a certain way
or put out my hand…

mist this morning over the ballfield
last night I left my coat
over a wooden banister

now I get colder while my coat
has nobody and no trouble

I hear that people are dying in America with the very

hot weather they're having
so I leap the waterslide

chest first and shout
it is the downliest way
water is a sympathetic institution

it corrects

the wrong drawn map
fords the creek over

illegible limestone
flows feral under the truck
I'm blind out here

landscape a green shroud

I write these tickets for myself
tear them into feathers

fashion precise swans I can't see
a negligible act
dismantled in the city that is only a perception

I'm a volunteer with this passenger pigeon

voice calling in aphonic ranges winter clue

from brush
a bluebird fire above the creek

It is the reverse of everything

backstage life
a costume held together with every kind of tape

black rubbed depth
or the adhesive that glows in thick sticks of gum
and an industry of Velcro

Periaktoi positioned on either side of the stage

three-sided posts revolve
to change one scene into another

interior to grounds-outside-the-palace
and turn again to rush in a coast
for all summer I sawed to build them

hung fresnel and ellipsoidal light in dark rafter

charmed the electrical cords
necessary sawing of two by fours

and stretching canvas over frames
realism necessary to craft fantasy
to fantasize the little society

turning of the image

privilege of the stagehand
theater alone with nothing

intimation of eternity cemetery-sacred
to get lost in possibility
each revolution of the set

a renewal

though I have forgotten for what play
I spent labor and then tore down

A dying man is almost grown

I'm holding a loaf of bread covered in tar
and then a record by my favorite band

her warm coat grew cold
I watched the thief led off by the elbow
after the king left

the king turned into a horse

his mistake was he trusted the hermit's words
my mistake is

I knocked the broom down with a stone
it is noon and shadows
land directly beneath their objects

laughter is shadow's ghost

sun brightest on top leaves
leaves a terrible army at rest

I'm on the porch in my underwear
watching all the bullshit hurry by

After the matinee I feel acutely

the ancient world
when I leave the movie theater for bright asphalt's

postcoital ease
parts of speech disbanded
usually nobody around

I'll see several movies in a row

without threat of having to pay twice
or be scolded

I watch movies until I say stop
these movies the earth watches

O to steady the language back on its feet
let it be my mother and father again

My name's in the forest

I want to rip paper
currency off the walls

build upon these misunderstandings
the garage man is missing
always

it begins when I leave the room

both directions out of house and body
I like the asps your eyes make

before I can get lightness
puppets tumble in the washer
I carry a few coins'

bright songs churning my pocket

tones of last gestures' terrible array
hungry to get bright cloud I'm headless

I carry a rock scoured white
why there's a driven word for it
and North American equivalent

a stop action uncertainty of markets

restlessly tying into consequence
the manner in which people talk

around a child
how my father
refuses to give his cat a name

whereas although my deficit is
I look into each thing

FIVE

From inside the secondhand store I admire

twenty amber ashtrays in the window
lacquer slathered on wooden lamps

hanging on to sun made ashtray-amber
by forest-fire smoke that has not cleared
the diminished sun replicated

on a thousand glosses glasses thimbles finishes

over the weekend a local man dies
traversing the window of a house he's trying to rob

on Mars the device continues to crawl
ash is falling from distant fires
north of town a man dressed as

Bigfoot is struck and killed

he's doing it for us
those who want to stay a little bit asleep

lean against pine until hillside forget
the airport's new luggage carousel

goes round like the rapids the city put
beneath the bridge to stimulate kayaking
and give mountain trolls

a riffle to wash their knuckles in

I am only dressed as a troll
although I don't remember

putting the heavy costume on
and can't find the zipper to take it off
not even the pimpled nose

or the one big tooth like the pawn ticket

a stranger gave me at the bus station
and I will someday get around to exchanging

when I have taken care of everything else
every other matter

In the industrial kitchen I take red debris from the dish

down to the houses of hot water and brush
steel and the epigrams of soap

the bubbles basket-edging
what giblets and tags of pasta
candlelit mouths reject

and leave behind

as diners drive to darkened kitchen
together and segue into sundry bedroom

or alone and stand at the sink and lie
I give back grinded to the sewers
skin-like skin of eggplant, spooned inside

the lamb bones bleated shut and opened

waking bright and clean I return
platters to their spinal stack

and in sterile silence hang
yellow gloves back on the ledge

In salmon silence of nineteen

although the prairies are burning
in faveolate lines

tonight's drive is more obscured in intention
than the road
this plan to get a room

and I would say make love

but looking back through smoke
I cannot see my own heart
writing its essay on heat

not virgins but virginal we unravel at the mouth

and the wine we bring is warm
and the bathroom is in the hall

and wake to a sunlight
that will save me the pleasure
of the heartbreak I'll later devour

Heartbreak, save me now, devouring pleasure!

In parenthood I am granted no respite from fear
I shine over formula bottle at my son

and will try to stack and store many years
ahead in natural calculation my face
the shape he'll need to see

uncertain in four a.m. fever

first nightmare blister broken arm and scare
save me from the terrible muscles of the hand

when he has become someone else

when he has become no one more
than compassion has transformed me to understand

Cottonwoods parse their shadows along the river

blanch
and one year do not break winter into leaf

so then say it was poetics that broke the singer's throat
and wash my hands in the morning sprinkler
while nurses ride up Brooks on bright yellow bikes

this morning I am like a truck driver

who stops in the middle of the road
walks back to check the lock and rub

some dust from the turn light
let that red warning through

and moseys in good weather back to the cab

hauls with one good arm
the heavy self back up to the wheel

The grill is wrapped tight against the autumn sprinkler

the lawn mowers are guttural cloistered and cloacal
like old gems polishing in the tumbler

or a furious air battle over a humanless sea
like one last air show pass
and all the children point

gasp—will he be all right? and the pilot leaps

I can't see the work from my room
where I keep the baby's calendar

try to be the first and last word
they are like waking from deep sick sleep
like the wrong body in the bed

the through time of loving electrical and ongoing

busy beneath the skin and deafened
it is why my son sleeps with one ear to my chest

and will soon stop thinking to
as language begins to fall apart midair

Above the canal tonight by the willow overhang

a jeep's trying to park
can't quite fit

grenade-skinned headlights reflect the surface
I think *under* it at first
a taxi turns mid-road lets three dudes off at a café

prophecy in the voice I stole

a narrative set sideways
up in my room I hear a bunch of guns

These on the other hand are orderly

little peaked roofs of boathouse row
they angle and tide throws higher

craft
a low bridge rises in the center
a kayak slides by a garish houseboat

quieting the shore

pale oars
dip short rhythm

a nurse soothing a patient
what to do with such pleasure
joined by slight bridges

I suppose
go home and make a child

The old man we pick up in Browning

coughs diesel and range
snow blocks us from fishing the reservoir

wiper blade waving as if to flag us down
a dog pisses on my tackle box at the Conoco
the guide who leads us here catches

fish like a covenant he's entered into

such mastery save me it doesn't him
halfway up another river the Lostine

trout lacquer over calico stone
early sparrow calls us together
into the tent which I zip up in one motion

yearling sets deer-heel

down in payment on flattest moss
like any river its job is to take away

It was my blanket first and she took it

harried weary at four a.m. and soda-pop high
because I'm American I can see

how to build from found objects
a really excellent bong
I have studied the purses of alchemy

deranged and precise as the Grand Canyon

I have undertaken to treat the adequate idea
I shall describe the sea

a little ways off a raven is croaking
every animal doing its weird thing
trembling weeds have grown since last rain

unless you touch them they will recite famous speeches

when the farmer wakes
streetlight then through the window

one makes money
tackling such frequencies
the alley ending its middle path on the pillow

eating raw reservoirs of anthem

among the ragged teachings of the field

what nation we had yesterday
remember how the sun felt

A train runs late through my arms

oranges ripen beside
the grudge match

although I have yet been born
aluminum this our small capital
a loyalty program until I lost home

astride though bright decay

after the shops close my shadow
ought to be your shadow

before the appetizers have even arrived
blind I did love the burn
swim out into gutter and glisten

that and the gas pumps and old billboard

that spring with the scarred hand
dog coming in from rain

Ospreys nest their rising dollars upright

search on their own and have no electricity
or heat or car no money

of their own
only my shadow under their right turns
how does the rest of it go

at lunch yesterday with Maria I said

experience is a repeating decimal
and she said well it wasn't at least

the steady movement out of the body's slipper
I nap and dream in portrait and landscape
sleep when the baby sleeps and ospreys spin

drifting off their nests grin sly subtleties

blotchy the wing storm-sympathetic
dives slavishly to talon bright scales

coho that twist as they silhouette away

I guess ospreys are tearing people apart too
something is

At the western outfitters the clerk

shows me a photo of the musk ox
he dropped near Kotzebue

his rifle a delicate woodwind
the car coat he sells is too much
blue as a bureau

handsome checkers and closed squares

wool rooms that would keep me
warm all century

instead I set forehead
hot against the window and watch
spring's first goose

land in the field the city set aside

soon the vista will be down

and to the south a gosling nothingness
my migrant eye already fevers

ABOUT THE AUTHOR

Ed Skoog was born in Topeka, Kansas, in 1971. He is the author of *Mister Skylight* (Copper Canyon Press, 2009). He has received fellowships from the Bread Loaf Writers' Conference, Lannan Foundation, Richard Hugo House, and the Jenny McKean Moore Writer in Washington Fellowship at George Washington University. He is currently a visiting professor at the University of Montana.

Lannan Literary Selections

For two decades Lannan Foundation has supported the publication and distribution of exceptional literary works. Copper Canyon Press gratefully acknowledges their support.

LANNAN LITERARY SELECTIONS 2013

Kerry James Evans, *Bangalore*

Sarah Lindsay, *Debt to the Bone-Eating Snotflower*

Lisa Olstein, *Little Stranger*

Roger Reeves, *King Me*

Ed Skoog, *Rough Day*

RECENT LANNAN LITERARY SELECTIONS FROM COPPER CANYON PRESS

James Arthur, *Charms Against Lightning*

Natalie Diaz, *When My Brother Was an Aztec*

Matthew Dickman and Michael Dickman, *50 American Plays*

Michael Dickman, *Flies*

Laura Kasischke, *Space, in Chains*

Deborah Landau, *The Last Usable Hour*

Michael McGriff, *Home Burial*

Heather McHugh, *Upgraded to Serious*

Valzhyna Mort, *Collected Body*

Lucia Perillo, *Inseminating the Elephant*

John Taggart, *Is Music: Selected Poems*

Tung-Hui Hu, *Greenhouses, Lighthouses*

Jean Valentine, *Break the Glass*

C.D. Wright, *One Big Self: An Investigation*

Dean Young, *Fall Higher*

For a complete list of Lannan Literary Selections from Copper Canyon Press, please visit Partners on our website: www.coppercanyonpress.org

 Poetry is vital to language and living. Since 1972, Copper Canyon Press has published extraordinary poetry from around the world to engage the imaginations and intellects of readers, writers, booksellers, librarians, teachers, students, and donors.

WE ARE GRATEFUL FOR THE MAJOR SUPPORT PROVIDED BY:

THE PAUL G. ALLEN
FAMILY FOUNDATION

Lannan

THE MAURER FAMILY
FOUNDATION

NATIONAL
ENDOWMENT
FOR THE ARTS

WASHINGTON STATE
ARTS COMMISSION

Anonymous

Arcadia Fund

John Branch

Diana and Jay Broze

Beroz Ferrell & The Point, LLC

Mimi Gardner Gates

Gull Industries, Inc.
on behalf of William and Ruth True

Mark Hamilton and Suzie Rapp

Carolyn and Robert Hedin

Steven Myron Holl

Rhoady and Jeanne Marie Lee

Maureen Lee and Mark Busto

New Mexico Community Foundation

H. Stewart Parker

Penny and Jerry Peabody

Joseph C. Roberts

Cynthia Lovelace Sears and Frank Buxton

The Seattle Foundation

Charles and Barbara Wright

The dedicated interns and faithful
volunteers of Copper Canyon Press

To learn more about underwriting Copper Canyon Press titles,
please call 360-385-4925 ext. 103

The Chinese character for poetry is made up of two parts:
"word" and "temple." It also serves as pressmark for
Copper Canyon Press.

The poems are set in Berthold Akzidenz Grotesk.
Book design and composition by Phil Kovacevich.
Printed on archival-quality paper at McNaughton & Gunn, Inc.